OUTLAW

BALLADS, LEGENDS & LORE
BY
WAYNE ERBSEN

*"I'm wild and woolly and full of fleas,
Never curried below my knees;
I'm a wild wolf,
And this is my night to howl."[1]*

Order No. NGB-500   ISBN: 1-883206-16-2

Contents

OUTLAW BALLADS, LEGENDS & LORE

Outlaws died hard. Though their bones were long ago laid to rest in Boot Hill graveyards, their legacy lives on in the ballads, the legends, and the lore.

Outlaws. The word itself seethes with visions of fierce and reckless desperados armed to the teeth and rushing headlong into trouble. This wild breed of men and women had their day in frontier America from the end of the Civil War until the 1890's. Like the hair triggers on their six-guns, they were walking sticks of dynamite, ready to explode without much notice. But outlaws were not alone in being edgy. Many of the men and women who ventured into the frontier had a restless spirit. Impetuous, fearless, not afraid to take risks...no wonder the West was wild! This independent breed of men and women often yielded to temptation to break the law in a land which scarcely had law. The timid stayed behind to mind the store.

Like the outlaws themselves, outlaw ballads pack a pretty fair punch. In lyrics and music they tell the unvarnished tales of daring and often tragic lives. Those who composed the ballads were far from impartial when wielding their pens. Many had a score to settle, a wrong to right, a moral to deliver.

Many of the outlaw songs had their roots in England and Ireland. These ancient ballads told tales of robbers, poachers, thieves and murderers who often paid for even minor crimes with their "heads." Like the badmen themselves, European ballads were restless and many traveled to America where they gained a new identity.

The outlaw ballads have helped to keep alive the memory of these bad men and women and the days in which they lived better than faded newspaper clippings, or dusty books. As long as they are sung, the outlaws live. Listen! You can hear the shooting, smell the gunsmoke, and taste the whiskey.

> *Outright Insult: If all his brains were dynamite, there wouldn't be enough to blow his nose.*

BAD LEE BROWN

Frontier Wisdom: If the saddle creaks, it's not paid for.

"**B**ad Lee Brown" is a finely crafted ballad which goes into all the lurid details of his crime, capture and conviction, but omits the minor detail of why he shot his victim in the first place. Popular around 1885, it has been collected in North Carolina, Tennessee, and Missouri as "Little Sadie," "Chain Gang Blues," "Penitentiary Blues" and "Out Last Night." John Lomax collected it simply as "Bad Man Ballad" from a tongue-tied Negro convict at Parchman, Mississippi. Some versions have the villain trying to escape to Mexico while others have it as "Jeryco."

Went out last night to take a little round
Met little Sadie and I blowed her down
Went back home, jumped into bed
Forty-four pistol under my head.

Woke up the next morning about half past nine
Hacks and the buggies a-standin' in line.
Gents and the gamblers standin' all around
Takin' little Sadie to her buryin' ground.

Then I got to studying of the deed I'd done
Grabbed my hat and away I run
Made a good run, but a little too slow
They overtook me in Jericho.

After a thief had been hanged, there came the painful duty of notifying his wife. Dice were thrown and the duty fell upon a gambler, who reluctantly knocked at the door of the ex-thief's cabin and asked:

"Does the widow Smith live here?"

"I'm Mrs. Smith," answered the woman, "but I am NOT a widow."

"I've got ten dollars that says you are.[4]"

Outright Insult:
He lasted as long as a pint of whiskey in a five-handed poker game.[12]

BAD LEE BROWN

"Montana's for bronc riders & hoss thieves; Texas is for russlers."

I was standin' on the corner readin' a bill,
Up stepped the sheriff, Mr. Thomas Hill,
Said, "Hey young man, ain't your name Brown,
Remember the night you shot Sadie down?"

I said, "Hey, yes sir, my name is Lee,
I murdered little Sadie in the first degree,
First degree, second degree,
Got any papers, won't you read 'em to me."

They took me downtown, dressed me in black,
Put me on the train and carried me back,
I had no friends to go my bail,
They crammed me back in the county jail.

LIFE AND MARVELOUS ADVENTURES
— OF —
WILD BILL,
THE SCOUT,
By J. W. BUEL, OF THE ST. LOUIS PRESS,
ILLUSTRATED WITH NUMEROUS ENGRAVINGS.

BEING A TRUE AND EXACT HISTORY OF ALL THE SANGUINARY COMBATS AND

HAIR-BREADTH ESCAPES OF THE MOST FAMOUS SCOUT AND SPY AMERICA EVER PRODUCED.

WILD BILL.

A marvelously exciting book, full of daring adventures and wonderful escapes among the Indians and lawless white men of the Far West.

PAPER COVERS, PRICE 25 CENTS.
Sent free to any address on receipt of price.
N. D. THOMPSON & CO., Publishers,
520, 522 and 524 Pine St., ST. LOUIS, MO.

The judge and the jury they took their stand,
The judge had the papers in his right hand,
Forty-one days, forty-one nights,
Forty-one years to wear the ball and stripes.

Now all young men take my advice:
Never take another poor girl's life,
It'll cause you to weep, cause you to mourn,
It'll cause you to leave your home sweet home.

Let a Sleeping Snake Lie

A sleeping outlaw woke up during the night to find something cold and heavy on his chest. As he stirred, he heard the whir of a rattlesnake, and in the dim moonlight he saw a blunt head with fangs bared, ready to strike. He knew that any sudden movement would be fatal. Very quietly he moved his hand toward his six-shooter, always placed within convenient reach. The snake was drawn into an "S," head erect. His hand closed on the butt of the six-shooter. He drew and fired just as the head was darting toward his face.

The outlaw paused. "What happened then?" asked his expectant listener. "I missed, so I went back to sleep."

BILLY THE KID

"I like to dance, but not in the air." Billy the Kid

The song "Billy the Kid" was written by Rev. Andrew Jenkins, who composed over eight hundred songs including "The Death of Floyd Collins," which was one of the most popular songs of the 1920's. Jenkins' other compositions also included "God Put a Rainbow in the Clouds" and "Ben Dewberry's Final Run." "Billy the Kid" was first recorded on February 15, 1927 by Vernon Dalhard.

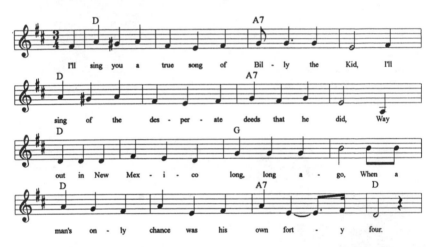

I'll sing you a true song of Bil - ly the Kid, I'll
sing of the des - per - ate deeds that he did, Way
out in New Mex - i - co long, long a - go, When a
man's on - ly chance was his own fort - y four.

When Billy the Kid was a very young lad,
In old Silver City he went to the bad.
Way out in the West with his gun in his hand,
At the age of twelve years, he killed his first man.

Fair Mexican maidens play guitars and sing
A song about Billy, their boy bandit king.
How ere his young manhood had reached its sad end
He'd a notch on his pistol for twenty-one men.

> **Outright Insult:**
> He was mean enough to hunt bears with a hickory switch.

BILLY THE KID

"Man's the only animal that can be skinned more'n once."

'Twas on the same night when poor Billy died,
He said to his friends, "I am not satisfied;
There are twenty-one men I have put bullets through,
And Sheriff Pat Garrett will make twenty-two."

Now this is how Billy the Kid met his fate:
The bright moon was shining, the hour was late,
Shot down by Pat Garrett, who once was his friend,
The young outlaw's life had come to an end.

There's many a man with a face fine and fair,
Who starts out in life with a chance to be square,
But just like poor Billy, he wanders astray,
And loses his life in the very same way.

Billy the Kid

The Kid could often be heard whistling
"Silver Threads Among the Gold," composed in 1873.

Billy the Kid - Fact or Fantasy

Myth: Billy the Kid was a Westerner.
Fact: He was born in New York City in 1859.
Myth: His name was William H. Bonney.
Fact: Billy's real name was Henry McCarthy.
Myth: He killed his first man at the age of twelve.
Fact: Billy was eighteen when he shot his first man.
Myth: Billy killed twenty-one men by the age of twenty-one.
Fact: He killed between eight to twelve men by that age.
Myth: Billy rescued a wagon train by routing the Indians with an axe.
Fact: Bald-face lie.
Myth: Billy rode 81 miles in 6 hours to spring a friend from jail.
Fact: A figment of Pat Garrett's imagination.
Myth: The Kid escaped to Mexico, where he died an old man.
Fact: Sheriff Pat Garrett killed the Kid with a single shot to the heart.

REWARD
(\$5,000.00)
Reward for the capture, dead or alive,
of one Wm. Wright, better known as

"BILLY THE KID"

Age, 18. Height, 5 feet, 3 inches.
Weight, 125 lbs. Light hair, blue
eyes and even features. He is
the leader of the worst band of
desperadoes the Territory has
ever had to deal with. The above
reward will be paid for his capture
or positive proof of his death.
JIM DALTON, Sheriff.

DEAD OR ALIVE!
BILLY THE KID

Weather Report
It was so hot and dry you'd had to prime yourself to spit.[12]

THE BOSTON BURGLAR

"All you need in this life is ignorance and confidence, and then success is sure." Mark Twain

"The Boston Burglar," a favorite around cowboy camp fires, was in fact a take-off on the British song "Botany Bay." The American version was credited to M. J. Fitzpatrick and copyrighted in 1881. H.J. Wehman first published it as a broadside, to be sold by newsboys on street corners. In 1885 Wehmam included it in *The Vocalist's Favorite Songster*. Not content to stay put, "The Boston Burglar," migrated back across the sea to Scotland and became "The Boston Smuggler."

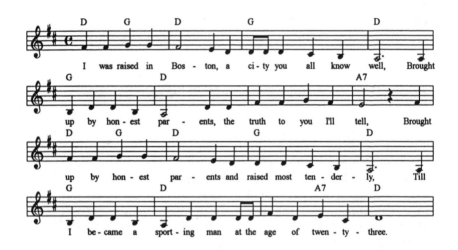

I was raised in Bos - ton, a ci - ty you all know well, Brought up by hon - est par - ents, the truth to you I'll tell, Brought up by hon - est par - ents and raised most ten - der - ly, Till I be - came a sport - ing man at the age of twen - ty - three.

Nervous?

Pat Garrett was asked if he was nervous when, in the dark, he shot and killed Billy the Kid. "No," he answered quickly. "A fellow with nerves wouldn't last long in the business I'm in."[1]

Outright Insult: He was meaner'n a sidewinder in a skillet.

The Boston Burglar

"When you fight with a skunk, you come out smelling a little."[24]

My character was taken and I was sent to jail,
My friends they found it all in vain to get me out on bail.
The jury found me guilty, the clerk he wrote it down,
The judge he passed the sentence and sent me to Charleston town.

I saw my aged father a-pleading at the bar,
I saw my dear old mother a-tearing out her hair,
Tearing out her old gray locks as the tears came streaming down,
Saying "Son, dear son, what have you done to be sent to Charleston town?"

They put me on an eastbound train one cold December day,
And as I passed the station I could hear the people say,
"Yonder goes a burglar, in strong chains he is bound,
For some great crime or other he is sent to Charleston town."

There is a girl in Boston, a girl that I love well,
And if ever I gain my liberty, a long life with her I'll dwell;
And when I gain my liberty, bad company I will shun,
Playing cards and gambling and also drinking rum.

To you who have your liberty, pray keep it while you can,
Don't walk around the streets at night, breaking the laws of man,
For if you do you'll surely rue and find yourself like me,
Serving out my twenty-one years in the state penitentiary.

Ready to Go??

A roving evangelist held a prayer meeting in Rowdy Kate's dance hall in Dodge City. Prairie Dog Dave sat suspiciously in the back of the crowded hall. In thundering tones the preacher finished his sermon with "Someday, boys, you are going to come to death's door, and you better be ready to go." Prairie Dog Dave arose and asked, "Do you mean to say you're ready to cash in any old time?" "Yes, sir, I am," answered the evangelist. "Then you better die right now, when you're settin' purty." With that, Prairie Dog pulled two six-shooters and banged away, not aiming to hit the preacher, but just for sport. As the bullets flew around the pulpit, the evangelist let out a yell and dove down behind some beer kegs. Prairie Dog blew smoke out of one of his guns and said, "Boys, you see? He's no more ready to die than I am."[1]

Outright Insult: He was so mad he could bite himself.

BULLY OF THE TOWN

Boot Hill Headstone: "Died of Lead Poisoning."

The curtains were pulled as May Irwin hit the stage of the Bijou Theater in New York City with a rousing version of "The Bully." The date was September 16, 1895, and the song was to be her trademark.

Among those who took credit for "The Bully" was sports writer Charles E. Trevathan who claimed he composed new lyrics to an old tune he learned from Tennessee blacks. It was likely Trevathan heard Mama Lou belt out "The Bully" at Babe Connor's brothel in St. Louis. At least four versions of "The Bully" were published in 1895, all prior to Trevathan's publication of the song. What *is* likely is that all these versions were based on an older traditional southern black song.

It was May Irwin's May 20, 1907 recording for Victor that helped spread the popularity of "The Bully." Old-time fiddlers played it as a snazzy instrumental, while southern singers sang a shortened version passed on by word-of-mouth or learned from the 1930's recordings by the likes of Mac and Bob, Byrd Moore, the Prairie Ramblers, Ernest Stoneman or Riley Puckett.

"The Bully" of 1895 was written in a heavy pseudo-Negro dialect, a practice wildly popular on the minstrel stage starting in the 1840's. In presenting this version one hundred years from its original publication date, I edited out all the inappropriate language and changed the last line of the chorus to match the line more commonly sung by early country entertainers of the early 1930's.

Just an Average Day

In one frontier town on a single day they had two street fights, hung a man, rode three men out of town on a rail, got up a quarter race, a turkey shoot, a gander pulling, a dog fight, and preaching by a circuit rider who afterwards ran a foot race for apple jack all around. And if this was not enough, the judge of the court, after losing his year's salary at single-handed poker and whipping a person who said he did not understand the game, went out and helped lynch his grandfather for hog stealing.[4]

BULLY OF THE TOWN

"It's sometimes safer to pull your freight than pull your gun."[12]

I'm a Tennessee rounder
And I don't allow,
No red-eyed river roustabout
With me to raise a row,
I'm looking for that bully
And I'll make him bow.

I'm going down the street
With my ax in my hand,
I'm lookin' for that bully
I'll sweep him off this land,
I'm looking for that bully
And he must be found.

Razors and guns a flyin'
Guns begin to squawk,
I lit upon that bully
Just like a sparrow hawk,
And that bully was just
A-dying to take a walk.

When you see me coming,
Hist your windows high,
When you see me goin,'
Hang your heads and cry,
I'm lookin' for that bully
And he must die.

Dodge City Whiskey

The run-of-the-bar whiskey in Dodge City was terrible stuff. The price was ten cents per glass, and the drinker poured. It was an insult not to fill the glass full, or to order something weaker than whiskey. Two or three glasses of this rot-gut was enough to make a man steal his own blankets.[22]

FRONTIER ETIQUETTE

Don't be too noisy about a man's past.
Never steal another man's horse.
Be hospitable to strangers.
Give your enemy a fighting chance.
Don't shoot an unarmed man.
Always fill your whiskey glass to the brim.
Do not practice ingratitude.
Defend yourself whenever necessary.
Look out for your own.
Remove your guns before sitting at the dining table.
Never order anything weaker than whiskey.
Don't make a threat without expecting dire consequences.

OUTLAW DENTISTRY

A fearless killer and dead shot, Clay Allison was suffering from a severe toothache. After riding two hundred miles, Allison found a dentist, who quickly pulled a tooth. When the ache didn't go away, Allison visited another dentist who observed, "Why, he pulled the **wrong tooth!**" The second dentist pulled the right tooth, and the ache was soon gone.

Allison celebrated with whiskey and returned to the office of the first dentist. Without saying a word, he grabbed him, flung him to the floor, and yanked out a molar and several front teeth. When he finished, he threw the forceps to the floor and asked, "How do you like your own medicine?"[1]

Outright Insult: He was crazy enough
to eat the devil with horns on.

COLE YOUNGER

"A loose hoss is always looking for new pastures."

For some, like Cole Younger, the Civil War never ended. A member of Quantrill's guerrillas and Shelby's Missouri Calvary, the war's end found Cole robbing banks and trains, often with his brothers Bob and Jim and Frank and Jesse James. In fact, the Younger and the James brothers carried out the first peacetime bank robbery in the United States in Liberty, Missouri on February 13, 1866. They also gained notoriety by a series of train robberies that set the model for the future robberies of John Dillinger, Pretty Boy Floyd and Clyde Barrow in the 1930's.

The Younger brothers' career as bank and train robbers was cut short during the failed attempt to rob the First National Bank in Northfield, Minnesota on September 7, 1876. Though the James brothers got away unharmed, all three Younger brothers were wounded and captured and sentenced to the penitentiary in Stillwater, Minnesota. Bob eventually died in prison, and Jim and Cole were paroled in 1901, after serving twenty-five years. The Youngers partly owed their release to the twenty-year-long efforts of W.C. Bronaugh, who was a Civil War veteran whose life Cole had saved back in 1862. After his release, Cole Younger earned his livelihood by joining Frank James lecturing on the evils of crime. They had finally made crime pay.

Even though the ballad "Cole Younger" was written as though it flowed from the pen of Cole Younger himself while confined in prison, such was not the case. It did, however, originate during the late 1870's or early 1880's, though its composer remains a mystery.

"Poor John, he has been hunted down and shot like a wild beast and never was a boy more innocent." – Cole Younger, talking about his late brother, who had been wanted for the murder of a deputy sheriff, whom he killed in a jailbreak.

Outright Insult: He was as drunk as a fiddler's clerk.

COLE YOUNGER

"Never run a bluff with a six-gun." Bat Masterson

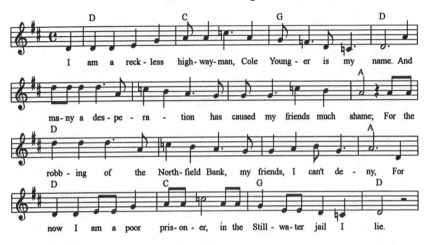

I am a reck-less high-way-man, Cole Young-er is my name. And many a des-pe-ra-tion has caused my friends much shame; For the robb-ing of the North-field Bank, my friends, I can't de-ny, For now I am a poor pris-on-er, in the Still-wa-ter jail I lie.

Read Ahead??

While in prison, Cole Younger had his "head read" by Dr. George Morris, who claimed he could tell a man's character by the bumps on his head. Known as phrenology, some late 19th century employers even insisted job applicants have their "heads read" before they could be hired.

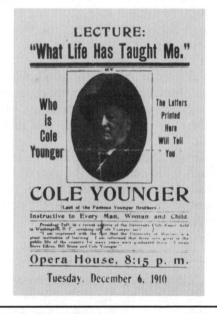

LECTURE:
"What Life Has Taught Me."

Who is Cole Younger

The Letters Printed Here Will Tell You

COLE YOUNGER
(Last of the Famous Younger Brothers.)

Instructive to Every Man, Woman and Child.

President Taft, in a recent address at the University Club dinner held in Washington, D. C., speaking of the Youngers said:
"I am impressed with the fact that the University at Missouri is a great institution of learning. I am informed that there were great in the public life of the country for many years were graduated there. I mean Steve Elkins, Bill Stone and Cole Younger."

Opera House, 8:15 p. m.

Tuesday, December 6, 1910

Coffee Anyone??

Legend tells how Clay Allison and Chuck Colbert stirred their coffee with the barrel of their six-shooters while facing each other across a table before a deadly gun fight.

COLE YOUNGER

"Colonel Colt made all men equal."

Of all my daring bold robberies a story to you I'll tell,
Of a California miner on whom my eyes befell;
I robbed him of his money and told him to go his way,
For which I will be sorry of until my dying day.

And then we started for Texas, where brother Bob did say,
That on fast horses we must ride in revenge of our father's day;
On them fast horses we did go to try to win the prize,
And we'll fight them anti-guerrillas until our dying day.

And the next we surprised was the Union Pacific train,
The crimes we done that bloody day brings tears into my eyes;
The engineer and fireman killed, the conductor escaped alive,
And now their bodies lie moulderin' beneath the Nebraska skies.

COLE YOUNGER

Then again we started for Texas, that good old Lone Star State,
A-crossin' the Nebraska prairies the James boys we did meet;
With guns and knives and revolvers we all sat down to play,
While drinkin' of good whiskey, boys, to pass the time away.

We saddled up our horses and northward we did go,
To that God-forsaken country that they call Minneso-ti-o,
We went to rob the Northfield bank and brother Bob did say,
"Now Cole, if you undertake this job you'll surely curse the day."

But I stationed out my pickets and up to the bank did go,
And there upon the counter I struck my fatal blow.
"Just hand us over your money, boys, and that without delay,
We are the famous Younger brothers, we spare no time to pray."

We got on our horses and we rode out of town
The lawmen pursued us and Jim was shot down.
Three of the brave companions made it home alive,
Three of the brave companions sleep beneath Minnesota skies.

---

*"Get your guns, boys! They're robbing the bank!" These words
alerted residents of the Northfield, Minnesota bank of the robbery
by the James-Younger Gang.*

DARLING COREY

"If I owned Hell and Texas I'd rent out Texas and live in Hell."
General William Tecumseh Sherman

Lest we believe that all the wild outlaws on the frontier were men, here's a song about Darling Corey, a gun totin', banjo playin', wine drinkin', barefooted, moonshinin' woman. Before the frontier was tamed, both men *and* women had to be pretty tough characters just to survive. Take Sal Fungus, for example. According to legend, she could "Scalp an Indian, laugh the bark off a pine tree, swim stark naked up a cataract, gouge out an alligator's eyes, dance a rock to pieces, sink a steamboat, blow out the moonlight, ride a panther bare-back, sing a wolf to sleep and scratch his hide off."[4] And that was **before** breakfast!

Wake up, wake up, dar-ling Cor-ey What makes you sleep so sound? The rev-e-nu - ers are a com-in' Gon-na tear yo-ur still - house down.

The first time I saw darling Corey,
She was standing on the banks of the sea.
With two pistols strapped around her body,
And a banjo on her knee.

The last time I saw darling Corey,
She had a wine glass in her hand,
She was drinkin' away her troubles
With a lowdown gambling man.

Go away, go away darling Corey,
Stop hanging around my bed.
Bad liquor destroyed my body;
Pretty women's gone to my head.

Dig a hole, dig a hole in the meadow,
Dig a hole in the cold, cold ground.
Dig a hole, dig a hole in the meadow,
Gonna lay darling Corey down.

> Outright Insult: He couldn't hit a bull's rump
> with a handful of banjos.[21]

DON'T LET YOUR DEAL GO DOWN

"I never killed unless I was compelled to." Belle Starr

"**D**on't Let Your Deal Go Down" was first recorded by Charlie Poole and the North Carolina Ramblers on July 27, 1925. Though not exactly an outlaw, Poole was constantly in scrapes with the law. Tales of run-ins with the law were legendary around Eden, North Carolina. One story tells of a policeman firing point blank at Poole's head. At the last second, Poole pulled his head back, and the bullet did some "instant dentistry" on his front teeth. Most publicity photos for Poole's successful recording career didn't show a big toothy grin.

Don't let your deal go do-wn, lit-tle girl,
Don't let your deal go down.
Don't let your deal go do-wn, lit-tle girl, 'Til your last go-ld dol-lar is gone.

I've been all around this whole wide world,
Been down to sunny Alabam'.
My mother said, "Now son don't go,
And never let your deal go down."

I'm going down to the railroad track.
Gonna take my rocking chair.
If those doggone blues don't leave my mind,
I'm gonna rock away from here.

My daddy was a railroad man,
Lived a mile and a half from here.
His head was found in a driver's wheel.
And his body has never been found.

> **"I never hanged a man—**
> **it was the law."**
> Judge Parker, the Hanging Judge

Painted on the outer walls of Billy Mensing's Kansas City saloon:
"IF DRINKING HURTS YOUR BUSINESS, QUIT YOUR BUSINESS."[1]

> Outright Insult: He looks so bad his ears flop.[12]

FRANKIE AND JOHNNY

"You can't fall out of bed if you sleep on the floor."

Frankie shot Johnny. Or was it Albert or Charlie or...? Folksong scholars have been brawling over the origins of this ballad for ages. Some say it can be traced to the ballad "Frankie Silvers," who was hung for murdering her husband Charlie with an axe as he lay sleeping in their cabin in the North Carolina mountains on December 22, 1831. Others claim, without much evidence, it was sung in Mississippi in the 1850's and during the siege of Vicksburg in 1863 during the Civil War.

Some evidence points to the October 15, 1899 shooting in St. Louis of Albert Britt by Frankie Baker as the crime that inspired the ballad "Frankie and Johnny." Early versions have been collected as "Frankie and Albert." In the late 1930's Frankie Baker sued Republic Pictures for $200,000 for releasing the movie "Frankie and Johnny." Frankie claimed the movie, which was based on the ballad, was a defamation of character. The judge was not impressed and threw out the case.

Frank-ie and John-ny were lov-ers, Oh, Lor-dy, how they could love. They swore to be true to each ot-her, Just as true as the stars a-bove, He's her man, but he do-ne he-r wrong.

In the early days of the West, cattle brands were frequently altered by cattle thieves. One cowboy, branded his cattle "B4." When he went to round up his cattle, they were all marked "B4U," and claimed by a nearby spread. The cowboy got even by branding every cow on the range "B4U2."[10]

Code of the West: "Shoot first, think and ask questions later."

FRANKIE AND JOHNNY

"Shoot first and never miss." Bat Masterson

Frankie went down to the corner, just for a bucket of beer,
She said, "Oh, Mr. Bartender, has my lovin' Johnny been here?"
He was her man, but he done her wrong.

"I don't want to cause you no trouble, I don't want to tell you no lie,
But I saw your lover half an hour ago, with a girl named Alice Bly,"
He was her man, but he done her wrong.

Frankie went down to the pawnshop, she bought herself a little forty-four,
She aimed it at the ceiling, and shot a big hole in the floor,
Where is my man, he's doin' me wrong.

Frankie went down to the hotel, she rang that hotel bell,
"Stand back all of you floozies or I'll blow you all to hell,"
I want my man, he's doin' me wrong.

Frankie threw back her kimono, she took out her forty-four,
Root-a-toot-toot, three times she shot, right through that hardwood floor,
She shot her man, 'cause he done her wrong.

"Roll me over easy, roll me over slow,
Roll me on my right side, 'cause the bullets hurts me so,
I was her man, but I've done her wrong."

"Oh bring on your rubber-tired hearses, bring on your rubber-tired hacks,
They're takin' Johnny to the graveyard, and they won't bring him back,"
He was her man, but he done her wrong.

"Oh, bring a thousand policemen, bring 'em right away,
Lock me down in the dungeon cell, and throw the keys away,"
I shot my man, 'cause he done me wrong.

Frankie said to the warden, "What are they goin' to do?"
The warden he said to Frankie, "It's the 'lectric chair for you,
You shot your man, tho' he done you wrong."

This story has no moral, this story has no end,
This story only goes to show that there ain't no good in men,
He was her man, and he done her wrong.

> He had a ten dollar Stetson on a five-cent head.[24]

THE GAMBLER

Never mention "rope" in the home of a hanged man.

The outlaw captured in the song was reportedly hung for murder in Fort Smith, Arkansas in the 1870's. If so, chances are good that he was sentenced to die by the famous hanging judge himself, The Honorable Isaac Charles Parker. From 1875 to 1896, Judge Parker had jurisdiction over Oklahoma and all of the Indian Territory. Over those twenty-one years, he tried over 13,500 cases and sentenced one hundred and sixty men to death. Of that number, seventy-nine were hanged during his term of office. During the first fourteen years he was on the bench, the convicted could seek no appeal, save from heaven.

Parker's chief executioner was George Maledon, who took great pride in his "scientific" hangings. Of the seventy-nine men sentenced to death by the Hanging Judge, Maledon personally hanged sixty. When he finally retired, he went on the lecture circuit, proudly displaying several of his hanging ropes.

The ballad sometimes entitled "I've Been All Around This World" has also been collected as "The Gambler," "My Father Was a Gambler," and "The New Railroad."

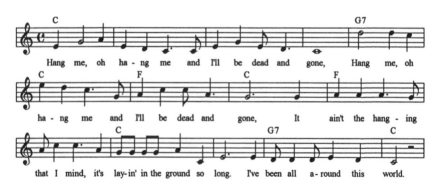

Hang me, oh ha-ng me and I'll be dead and gone, Hang me, oh ha-ng me and I'll be dead and gone, It ain't the hang-ing that I mind, it's lay-in' in the ground so long. I've been all a-round this world.

"Everything's quiet in Cimarron.
Nobody's been killed for three days."

THE GAMBLER

My father was a gambler, he taught me how to play,
My father was a gambler, he taught me how to play.
Sayin' "Son don't go a-begging while you've got the ace and trey,"
I've been all around this world.

Up on the Osage mountains where the wind blows chilly and cold,
Up on the Osage mountains where the wind blows chilly and cold,
Where I hid out last winter, starved and nearly froze,
I've been all around this world.

Up on the Osage mountains, it's there I make my stand,
Up on the Osage mountains, it's there I make my stand,
With a rifle on my shoulder, a six-shooter in my hand,
I've been all around this world.

> **Outlaw Nick-Names**
>
> *Slim Kid, One-Shot Charlie, Chicken, Skeeter, Wild Dick, Black-Faced Charlie, Indian Bob, Long Gordon, Tulsa Jack, Dynamite Dick, Blue Duck, Rattlesnake Charlie.*

Lulu, oh Lulu, come and open up the door,
Lulu, oh Lulu, come and open up the door,
Before I have to open it with my old .44,
I've been all around this world.

There's mama and papa, little sister she makes three,
There's mama and papa, little sister she makes three,
To follow me down to the gallows and see the last of me,
I've been all around this world.

The railroad is finished, the cars are on the track,
The railroad is finished, the cars are on the track,
Just telegraph the news to mama, her money will bring me back,
I've been all around this world.

BELLE STARR

Outright Insult: He was meaner'n a new-sheared sheep.[12]

THE HANGMAN

The origins of "Hangman" can be traced to the ballad "The Maid Freed From the Gallows," which was based on events that took place in old England over 500 years ago. Some whispered that the king's affections had been spurned by one of his own young servant women. As punishment, the King stole a golden ball from the Queen and planted it among the servant's possessions. Accused of theft, she was sentenced to hang. Moments before her execution, she spied members of her family who came to watch her hang. Following the "father" verse, you can add "mother," "sister," and brother." At long last, her sweetheart shows up to save the day.

Hang - man, Hang - man, slack your rope Slack it for a while For yon - der comes my fath - er dear Whose tra - veled for ma - ny a mile.

Father, Oh father, have you brought me gold,
Have you come to set me free?
Or have you come to see me hung,
Beneath the gallows tree?

Daughter, Oh daughter, I've not brought you gold,
I have not come to set you free,
But I have come to see you hung,
Beneath the gallows tree.

Sweetheart, sweetheart, have you brought me gold,
Any gold to pay my fee?
Or have you come to see me hung,
Upon the gallows tree?

Sweetheart, dear sweetheart, I've brought the gold,
I've come to set you free,
I have not come to see you hung,
Upon the gallows tree.

"His double-barrel shotgun wasn't loaded with sofa pillars."

THE HIGHWAYMAN

"He looked like death on a cracker."

"The Hangman" and "The Highwayman" offer a fascinating look into just how completely a ballad can change over time. Both started out as a ballad about a single event. "The Hangman" is now commonly sung in a minor key, in 2/4 time, while "The Highwayman" is sung in a major key, in 3/4 time. The chorus of "The Highwayman" consists of singing the last line of the previous verse twice followed by the third and fourth lines of that verse.

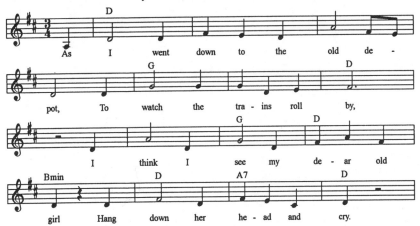

The night was dark and stormy,
It surely looked like rain.
Not a friend in this whole wide world
Nobody knew my name.

Wait, Mr. Judge, oh, wait, Mr. Judge,
Wait a little while.
I think I saw my dear old girl
She's walked for miles and miles.

Dear girl, have you brought me silver?
Dear girl, have you brought me gold?
Or have you walked these long, long miles
To see me hanged upon the hangman's pole

Dear boy, I've brought you silver,
Dear boy, I've brought you gold.
I have not walked these long, long miles
To see you hanged upon a hangman's pole.

She took me from the scaffold
She untied my hands.
Tears rolled down that poor girl's cheeks
"I love that highwayman."

> "You're the sickest looking lot of sheriffs I ever seen."
> Tom Horn's comments as he mounted the gallows.

JESSE JAMES

"I have lived as a respectable citizen and obeyed the laws of the United States to the best of my knowledge." Letter by Jesse James, printed in Liberty Tribune, July 15, 1870.

Frank James, Shoe Salesman??

In his later years, Frank James was hired by Sanger Brothers department store in Dallas, Texas as a shoe salesman. When the word got out, Sangers' was jammed with curiosity-seekers wanting to catch a glimpse of the famous ex-outlaw.

One day, a big, gruff bully barged his way into the shoe department at Sangers'. Waiting on him was the well-dressed, soft-spoken Frank James. After boisterously ordering the salesman around, the bully threatened him, saying, "Do you know who I am? I'm Bill Duggans and I've got a mind to bust you up-side the head if you don't find me the boots I want." "Mr. Duggans, do you know who *I* am?" "No, who *are* you?" "I'm Frank James. Perhaps you've heard of me and my Brother, Jesse." With that, the bully's face grew pale, his knees began to tremble, and through clenched teeth and a forced smile he said meekly, "I like these here boots 'jes fine, and if it's all right with you, I'll take 'em," and he left the store in a big hurry.[9]

"When I'm done with you, there won't be enough left of you to snore."

JESSE JAMES

"I have harmed no man and taken nothing from no man."
Jesse James, October 15, 1872.

His friends called him "Dingus," but you and I know him as Jesse James, America's most famous outlaw. When the Civil War began, Missouri's sentiments were split between the Confederacy and the Union. Frank James quickly joined the Confederacy. His younger brother Jesse, though only thirteen and a half, was itching to fight. He soon got his chance by joining Bloody Bill Anderson and William Clarke Quadrill and their band of pro-Confederate guerrillas as they wreaked havoc over much of Missouri and Kansas. By the war's end, the James brothers were not yet ready to quit fighting; they still had a score to settle.

The Missouri that Frank and Jesse found when they returned home from the war was not the same place they left five years earlier. To them, Missouri had become overrun with carpetbaggers, radicals, and Union sympathizers. Denied amnesty as Missouri guerrillas, Frank and Jesse turned their wrath from fighting Yankees to looting banks and trains. Between 1866 and 1882 they held up twelve banks, seven trains and five stagecoaches in eleven states and territories for a total haul approaching a half a million dollars. In the process, they carried out the first peacetime train robbery and the first daytime bank robbery.

Though relentlessly hunted by sheriffs, Pinkertons, railroad detectives and posses, Frank and Jesse managed to escape capture. For many rural Missouri residents, in fact, they became folk heroes, "robbing the rich and giving to the poor." They certainly robbed the richest banks and trains because that's where the money was. Though there is no evidence that the James boys ever gave to the poor, they became heroes to many rural Missouri residents who hated railroads and banks for robbing *them*.

Jesse's Revenge

Even in death, Jesse was able to ruin the political career of Gov. Thomas T. Crittenden, who put up the $10,000 for Jesse's murder. Criticized by his own Democratic party, he lost the bid for reelection and was rejected by President Cleveland for a diplomatic post.

JESSE JAMES

"Jesse W. James is America's Robin Hood."
Theodore Roosevelt

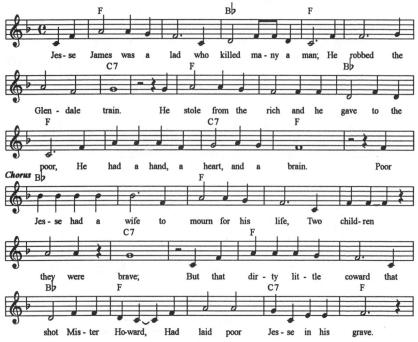

Jes-se James was a lad who killed ma-ny a man; He robbed the Glen-dale train. He stole from the rich and he gave to the poor, He had a hand, a heart, and a brain. Poor

Chorus

Jes-se had a wife to mourn for his life, Two child-ren they were brave; But that dir-ty lit-tle coward that shot Mis-ter Ho-ward, Had laid poor Jes-se in his grave.

With his brother Frank they robbed the Gallatin bank,
They carried the money from the town.
And in this very place they had a little race,
For they shot Captain Sheets to the ground.

It was on a Wednesday night, the moon was shining bright,
They robbed the Glendale train.
And the people they did say for many miles away,
It was robbed by Frank and Jesse James.

Newspaper Headlines

"Goodbye, Jesse!"   "Jesse James Killed"
"Jessie is Dead"   "The Dead Outlaw"

"Why didn't they just work?" Rita Erbsen, age 9.

JESSE JAMES

"I want results when I fight." Frank James

They went to a crossing not very far from there,
And here, once again, they did the same.
With the agent on his knees, he delivered up the keys,
To Frank and his brother Jesse James.

It was that Robert Ford, the dirty little coward,
I wonder how he does feel.
For he ate of Jesse's bread and he slept in Jesse's bed,
Then he laid Jesse James in his grave.

It was on a Saturday night, poor Jesse was at home,
Talking to his family brave.
Robert Ford watched his eye, and shot him on the sly,
And he laid Jesse James in his grave.

Courtesy of Jim Bob Tinsley

REPUTED TO BE JESSE JAMES.
IT WASN'T

COURTESY OF JIM BOB TINSLEY

JESSE JAMES AT AGE
SEVENTEEN.

The people held their breath when they heard of Jesse's death,
And wondered how he ever came to die.
Robert Ford's pistol ball brought him tumbling from the wall,
For he shot poor Jesse on the sly.

Jesse went to his rest with his hand upon his breast,
The Devil will be down upon his knee.
He was born one day in the county of Clay,
And he came from a solitary race.

This song was made by Billy Gashade,
Just as soon as the news did arrive.
He said there was no man with the law in his hand
That could take Jesse James when alive.

Due to the exploits of Jesse James and his gang, national news-
papers branded Missouri, "The Outlaw State," "Poor Old Missouri,"
"The Robber State," "The Outlaw's Paradise," and "Heaven For
Outlaws." As a result, immigration to Missouri suffered.

"A man's a fool to drink. It takes away his money and his brains." Frank James

JOHN HARDY

The six-shooter was judge, jury and executioner.

It was pay-day night at the Shawnee Coal Company in McDowell County, West Virginia in 1893. John Hardy was celebrating by gambling and drinking heavily. During a crap game John laid his pistol on the table and solemnly spoke to his gun: "Now, I want you to lay here. The first man that steals money from me, I mean to kill him." About midnight he began to lose, and claimed that one of the players had stolen twenty-five cents from him. Denying that he had taken the money, the accused man took one look at John Hardy's weapon, and gave him twenty-five cents. With that, John Hardy said, "Don't you know that I won't lie to my gun," and shot the man dead.

Captured while asleep by Sheriff John Effler and deputy John Campbell, John Hardy was brought to jail to stand trial for murder. He was convicted and sentenced to die on January 19, 1894. On the gallows he told the large throng who came to witness the execution that he had gotten religion, and warned all men to avoid gambling and whiskey.

The melody of this unusual version was collected from Delie Norton of Sodom Laurel, North Carolina by David Holt. The words were printed in *The Sunday Advertiser,* Huntington, West Virginia, April 29, 1923.

John Har - dy was a des - per - ate lit - tle man, He car - ried two guns eve - ry day He killed a man in a Sha - w - ne - e camp; You ought to see John Har - dy get - tin' a - way, po - or boy, You ought to see John Har - dy get - tin' a - way.

Outright Insult: If he closed one eye he'd look like a needle.[12]

JOHN HARDY

John Hardy was standing at the bar-room door,
Showing no interest in the game.
Up stepped a woman with a dollar in her hand,
Saying, "Deal John Hardy in the game, poor boy,
Deal John Hardy in the game."

John Hardy took that little woman's money,
And then began to play.
Saying, "The man that wins my little woman's dollar,
John Hardy will blow him away, poor boy,
And lay him in his lonesome grave."

Just before Boone Helm was hanged in Virginia City, Montana in 1863, he yelled out, "Every man for his principles. Hurrah for Jeff Davis!" He then kicked the box from under his feet and died by his own foot![11]

A Texas cowboy denied stealing a horse and pleaded not guilty in court. His lawyer managed to get him off, and he was set free by the judge. As he was leaving the court-room, the cowboy turned back to the judge with a puzzled look.
"Judge," he asked, "Does this mean I can keep the hoss?"[7]

John Hardy made for the Coalburg train,
It was so dark he could hardly see.
Up stepped the constable and took him by the arm,
"Johnny won't you come and go with me, poor boy,
Johnny won't you come and go with me."

I been to the East and I've been to the West,
I've been this wide world 'round.
I've been to the river and I've been baptized,
And now I'm on my hanging ground, poor boy,
Now I'm on my hanging ground.

They took him to the scaffold high,
They hung him there to die.
The last words that John Hardy said,
"My forty-four never lies, poor boy,
My forty-four never lies."

Courtesy of Jim Bob Tinsley

Wild Bill Hickok is fifth from left.

"He was as dead as a can of corned beef."

LILLY OF THE WEST

"Laws Sometimes Sleep, But Never Die."
From a Chinese fortune cookie.

Singing can be downright hazardous to your health, or so it was for the victim in this haunting ballad, "The Lilly of the West." The poor fool who committed the dastardly deed was driven to temporary madness by lovely Flora, who betrayed him. Yet in the end, stupidity prevailed and he loved her still.

Originally a British ballad, "The Lilly of the West" was published in *The Dime Songster* (Indianapolis, 1859), *Beadle's Dime Songster* (New York, 1860) and *Uncle Sam's Army Songster* (Indianapolis, 1862). Early folk song collectors found it in Kentucky, North Carolina, Missouri, Arkansas and even Nova Scotia. In some versions, the villainess Flora becomes Mary and Louisville becomes Michigan or Louisiana.

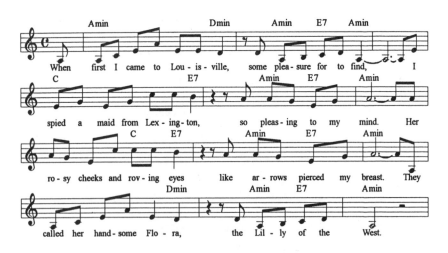

When first I came to Lou-is-ville, some plea-sure for to find, I spied a maid from Lex-ing-ton, so pleas-ing to my mind. Her ro-sy cheeks and rov-ing eyes like ar-rows pierced my breast. They called her hand-some Flo-ra, the Lil-ly of the West.

The Legend of Boot Hill
The famed graveyard started when a friendless cowboy was killed in a gunfight on a hill overlooking Dodge City. Still wearing his boots, he was wrapped in a blanket and buried where he fell.

LILLY OF THE WEST

Always carry your plug of tobacco in the pocket opposite your six-shooter so your enemies will know what you're reaching for.

I courted her for many a day, some favors for to gain,
But she turned her back upon me, which caused me grief and pain.
She robbed me of my liberty, deprived me of my rest,
But still I loved my Flora, the Lilly of the West.

One evening as I rambled, down by yonder shady grove,
I saw a man of high degree conversing with my love.
He sang, he sang so merrily that I was sore oppressed,
He sang for lovely Flora, the Lilly of the West.

I rushed up to my rival, a dagger in my hand,
I caught him by the collar and boldly bid him stand.
Being mad to desperation, my dagger pierced his breast,
I was betrayed by Flora, the Lilly of the West.

I had to stand my trial, and I boldly made my plea,
They put me in a criminal box and there convicted me.
Though she robbed me of my liberty, deprived me of my rest,
But still I love my Flora, the Lilly of the West.

On a drunken binge, wild man Clay Allison raced and war-whooped his horse through town wearing ONLY his boots.

Messin' With the Law

A new ballad by that no-good outlaw, Wayne Erbsen.

Jim said "Wayne we've got to go and fix that wound of yours. A
bul-let in the leg just can't do you no good. The
doc 'll patch you up and then we've got to ride, The
sher-iff's on our trail, boys, a-cross the Great Div-ide.

Two more miles to go, boys, and Mexico's our goal,
The pretty senoritas will make us feel at home.
Our saddle bags are full of the gold that we stole,
It'll last a long, long time, boys, down in Mexico.

Just before we crossed the border, I fell down from my horse,
I was so weak from loss of blood, I could not go no more.
Jim just kept on ridin', the gold was in his sack,
I raised my forty-four, boys, and shot him in the back.

I layed there in the desert sand, the Lord knows for how long,
I knew my time had come to die for living so doggone wrong.
High above the mesa, I heard an awful sound,
A lynch mob come to take me to my hangin' ground.

I never thought I'd smile to see the sheriff's ugly face,
The circuit judge must hear my pleas, though I'll not confess.
I'd rather rot in prison for the rest of my days,
Than to face the hangman's noose for all my rowdy ways.

The sheriff's men took hold of me and to my great surprise,
They tied a rope around me neck, and blindfolded my eyes.
Then they kicked away my footin', and I commenced to fall,
My soul will burn in Hell, boys, for messin' with the law.

THE STRANGE CAREER OF BLACK BART

Seldom had the West seen an outlaw quite like Black Bart. To his friends in high society San Francisco in the 1870's, he was Charles Bolton, polite, well-mannered, and a prefect gentleman. He was often seen about town in a dapper three-piece suit and sporting a bowler hat. He counted as his friends some of San Francisco's most respected citizens, including a number of noted police officers and city officials. His profession, they thought, was that of a prosperous mine owner.

The *other* Charles Bolton was ex-Confederate soldier Charles E. Boles, alias Black Bart, "P o 8" (poet). For eight years he vexed Wells Fargo detectives by committing twenty-eight stage robberies. To his credit, he never fired a shot from his unloaded shotgun, and never harmed or robbed a single passenger. His trademarks included always working alone on foot, wearing a flour-sack mask, and his ever-polite demand that the stage driver, **"PLEASE THROW DOWN THE BOX."** His identity was finally revealed when it was discovered that his handkerchief lost during a holdup bore a Chinese laundry mark, which led to his arrest and conviction. After at least two of his robberies he left a poem signed, "Black Bart, the P o 8."

BLACK BART

Here I lay me down to sleep
To wait the coming morrow
Perhaps success, perhaps defeat
And everlasting sorrow.
Let come what will, I'll try it on
My condition can't be worse,
And if there's money in the box,
It's munny in my purse.
                    Black Bart, the P o 8

I've labored long and hard for bread
For honor and for riches
But on my corns too long you've tread
You fine haired sons of bitches.
                    Black Bart, the P o 8

THE OLD MAID AND THE BURGLAR

"Never speak loudly unless your shanty is on fire."

Old maids have been the brunt of jokes since the day marriage was invented. This hilarious song is seen through the eyes of a burglar who watches from under a bed as the old lady he is set to rob removes various body parts, including her wig, glass eye and teeth. Originally entitled "The Old Maid's Last Hope," it is credited to E.S. Thilp, 1887.

I'll tell you a sto - ry of a bur - g - lar man Who went to rob a house. Went in the win - dow, crawled un - der the bed, Just as qui - et - ly as a mouse.——

He was thinking of some money to get,
While under the bed he lay,
The burglar saw a sight that night
That made his hair turn grey.

About nine o'clock an old maid came in,
"I am so tired," she said.
Glad to see her home was well,
She forgot to peep under the bed.

She took out her teeth & the big glass eye,
And the hair right off of her head.
That burglar man had nineteen fits
As he rolled out from under her bed.

From under the bed this burglar came,
He was a total wreck.
The old maid didn't holler at all
But she grabbed him 'round the neck.

Then from her bosom a revolver she drew,
And to this burglar man said:
"You'll marry me, you burglar man,
Or I'll blow off the top of your head."

He looked at the teeth and the big glass eye,
And he had no place to scoot,
He looked back at the bald-headed miss
Said, "Woman, for the Lord's sake, shoot!"

> "I never hanged a man that didn't deserve it."
> George Maledon, Judge Parker's hangman.

Nuthin' to Steal

A newcomer was being tried in kangaroo court for coming to Texas.
The defendant was asked, "Why did you leave Georgia?"

"I thought Texas was a better country."

"Come on, let's have the truth. Did you shoot somebody?"

"No."

"Did you steal a horse?"

"No."

"Did you steal anything?"

"No."

"Then why didn't you steal anything?"

"Because the fellows who had already come to Texas hadn't left anything worth stealin'."[4]

CAPTAIN JOHN JARRETT

Raised in a canebreak,
Fed in a hog trough,
Suckled by a she-bear
The click of a six-shooter is music
to my ear!
Wh-o-o-o-p-e-e!
The further up the creek you go
The worse they get,
An' I come from the head of it!
Wh-o-o-o-p-e-e!
Born high up on the Guadalupe,
Raised on a thorny prickly pear,
Quarrelled with alligators,
And fought grizzly bears.[20]

He'd been in the desert so long,
he knew all the lizards by their first names.

Old Hatfield Recipe Fruit Cake

collected by Mary Hall

For Outlaws and Inlaws

3 cups white sugar	3 1/4 cups cold water
1 lb. dark raisins	1 1/4 cups butter
1 lb. light raisins	1 tsp. each: cinnamon, nutmeg, cloves, allspice and salt

Boil the above ingredients together five minutes. When cold, add: 1 large box chopped dates, 8 oz. dried fruit (optional) 2 jars red cherries well drained (optional), 4 cups coursely chopped nuts (save some for top of cake), 3 teaspoons soda - dissolve in a bit of cold water, 7 cups of flour - mix well.

Grease flu (flutted) pan and large loaf pan. Line with wax paper and grease it too. Add nuts and cherries to tops of cakes just before putting in oven.

Bake in preheated oven at 300° for 1.5 hours. Test with toothpick. When done, let stand for 25 minutes. Turn out on plate. Remove wax paper; then turn cake upright again.

Soak a washed unbleached muslin cloth with brandy and wrap it around cake. Cover tightly.[23]

It was so dry the bushes followed the dogs around.

OTTO WOOD THE BANDIT

"Old Judge Colt was the final arbiter of all disputes."

The life of Otto Wood was the stuff dime novels were made of. Born in Wilkes County, North Carolina on May 9, 1894, Otto ran away from home at just seven years old. After stealing rides aboard several passenger trains, he lived for a time in West Virginia with the infamous Hatfield clan who were engaged in deadly feuds with their sworn enemies, the McCoys. From the Hatfields, Otto learned the skills that would later become his stock and trade: moonshining, gambling, and shooting.

At the age of thirteen, he committed his first crime — stealing a bicycle, which he hadn't even learned to ride. When finally shot down at the age of thirty-seven in a running gun battle with the sheriff of Salisbury, North Carolina, Otto Wood had become the most notorious outlaw North Carolina had ever known. His exploits included having made no less than ten daring escapes from prison. He was wanted in at least six states for car and horse theft, moonshining and murder.

Otto was a man you didn't mess with. Once on the lam in the Southwestern desert, he fought off a pack of wolves and then captured a gang of Mexican outlaws who were trying to rob him. Otto turned the surprised thieves over to the law, but didn't stick around to claim the reward for fear of being recognized and sent back to prison. His most notorious crime was the November 3, 1923 murder of A. W. Kaplan, a Greensboro, North Carolina pawnbroker. They apparently quarrelled when Otto discovered that his father's pocket watch, which he had pawned, had been sold.

The ballad "Otto Wood the Bandit" was composed by Walter "Kid" Smith and recorded in New York City not over a month after Wood was slain on January 1, 1931.

How to Disarm an Outlaw

First, get the drop on him. Without relaxing vigilance, command him to unbuckle his gun belt in front, and let it and its six-shooters fall to the ground. Then force the outlaw to step away from his weapon far enough for the officer to safely pick it up and march the prisoner off to jail.[1]

37

OTTO WOOD THE BANDIT

"OTTO WOOD SLAIN," *Greensboro Daily News*, January 1, 1931

Step up bud-dy and lis-ten to my song, I'll sing it to you right, but you
might sing it wrong. It's all a-bout a man named Ot-to Wood, I
can't tell you all, but I wish I could. Ot-to why
didn't you run, Ot-to's done dead and gone. Ot-to why
didn't you run, When the sher-iff pulled out his for-ty four gun.

He walked in a pawnshop a rainy day,
And with a clerk he had a quarrel they say.
He pulled out a gun and he struck a fatal blow
And this is the way the story goes.

> *"It does not pay to dodge the law." Otto Wood*

They spread the news as fast as they could,
The sheriff served a warrant on Otto Wood.
The jury said murder in the second degree,
Then judge passed sentence to the penitentiary.

They put him in the pen, but it done no good,
It couldn't hold a man called Otto Wood.
It wasn't very long 'til he slipped outside,
Pulled a gun on a guard said, "Take me for a ride."

OTTO WOOD IN PRISON, 1926

> *"There is only one road away from trouble, and this is along the straight and narrow road." From THE LIFE OF OTTO WOOD, by Otto Wood. (Written in prison, 1926).*

Outright Insult: He's so mean he'd steal a fly
from a blind spider.[24]

OTTO WOOD THE BANDIT

"Wild and woolly, hard to curry."[11]

The second time they caught him was away out West,
In a holdup gang he got shot through the breast,
They brought him back and when he got well,
They locked him down in the dungeon cell.

He was a man who would not run,
He always carried a .44 gun.
He loved the women and he hated the law,
And he just wouldn't take noboby's jaw.

He rambled out West, and he rambled all around,
He met two sherriffs in a Southern town.
The sheriff said, "Otto step to the way,
'Cause I've been expecting you every day."

He pulled out his gun and then he said,
"Make a crooked move and you'll both fall dead.
Crank up your car and take me out of town,"
But a few minutes later, he was graveyard bound.

Courtesy of Mary Ingram

OTTO WOOD

Outlaw's Code: Draw quick and shoot straight.
Lawman's Code: Take your time and shoot straight.

Poor Rounder

"Bill Thompson was quarrelsome when drunk, and he was nearly always drunk."[1]

If a song could be called a "vagabond," "Poor Rambler" would certainly qualify. It has wandered around the country, picking up stray bits of "Darling Cory," "Country Blues," "Little Maggie," and "Goin' to Georgia."

Come all you good time peo_____ple, While_ I have mon - ey to spend. To - mor - row might be Mon___day, And I nei - ther . have a dol - lar or a friend.

When I had plenty of money,
My friends were all standing around,
But as soon as my pockets were empty
Not a friend on this earth could be found.

And it's all around this jailhouse,
Forty dollars will pay my fine,
Corn licker's around in my body
Pretty women are troublin' my mind.

If I had a listened to my mama,
I wouldn't a' been here today,
A lyin' around this jailhouse
Just sleeping my life all away.

Give me cornbread when I'm hungry,
Give me whiskey when I'm dry,
Give me greenbacks when I'm hard up
Sweet Heaven when I die.

Dig a hole, dig a hole in the meadow,
Dig a hole in the cold, cold ground,
Go and dig me a hole in the meadow
And just watch this poor rounder go down.

Why Three Shots?

Sheriff Ben Thompson of Austin, Texas was asked why he had fired three shots in a gun fight with a notorious outlaw when the first shot had killed him. "The first shot was to make him fall; the second was a precaution in case the first did not finish him off. The third was to scare his gang in the saloon."

DEATH BY OVEREXPOSURE

Fly-Speck Bill, horse thief and murderer, was introduced to a vigilante's rope one bitterly cold winter night. The committee, fearing trouble with the law, was at the coroner's the next morning and asked if he would be so kind as to square things when he made his report.

"Well, I don't know, boys," the coroner replied. 'Did you leave Bill hangin' there in that tree all night?"

"Yup."

"That being the case," said the coroner, "Old Fly-Speck sure would have frozen to death if he hadn't got his neck busted. I reckon I'll jes' have to report he died from 'overexposure."[7]

LACK OF EVIDENCE

A man who had killed a gambler in a game of poker stood before the justice of the peace, who asked, "Are you guilty or not of downing this man?"

"Guilty."

"What did you kill him for?"

"He started to count the cards in the deck."

"Suspected him of cheating, eh?"

"Sure. He might just as well have come right out and accused me of cheating."

"That's so. Who saw you down this man?"

"No one, we was playing alone."

"Then go on about your business and keep your mouth shet. Prisoner is discharged for lack of evidence."[7]

"Licker talks mighty loud when it gits loose from the jug."
Joel Chandler Harris

Courtesy of Jim Bob Tinsley

Texas Ranger Bill McDonald
"He would charge hell with a bucket of water."

Only One Riot

A gang of cowboys went on a riot in a Texas town, shot out the lights and windows, killed several citizens and terrorized the town. A call was sent to Austin for the Texas Rangers to come and quell the outbreak.

Ranger Pat Dooling showed up alone. When he got off the train, the town officials were looking around for the other rangers. "I'm the ranger," said Dooling. "Did they only send ONE Ranger?" "You've only got one riot, haven't you?" asked Dooling. He soon quelled the riot and boarded the next train.[1]

Outright Insult: He was mad enough to swallow
a horn-toad backwards.[21]

QUANTRILL

A former Bible-school teacher, William Clarke Quantrill, was wanted by 1859 as a horse thief, slave stealer, and murderer. He soon joined the Confederacy and recruited a band of 450 guerrillas that included Jim Younger, Cole Younger, Frank James and Jesse James. In an act of revenge and hatred, Quantrill and his raiders looted and burned Lawrence, Kansas, murdering 150 citizens in August of 1863. This badly biased ballad was written by one of his unknown supporters.

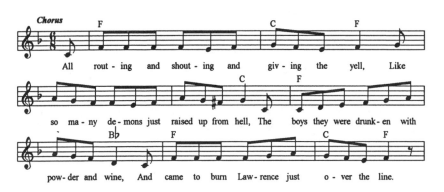

All rout-ing and shout-ing and giv-ing the yell, Like so ma-ny de-mons just raised up from hell, The boys they were drunk-en with pow-der and wine, And came to burn Law-rence just o-ver the line.

Come all you bold robbers
And open your ears,
Of Quantrill the lion heart
You quickly shall hear.
With his band of bold raiders
In double-quick time,
He came to burn Lawrence
Just over the line.

They came to burn Lawrence,
They came not to stay,
They rode in one morning
At breaking of day,
With guns all a-waving
And horses all foam,
And Quantrill a-riding
His famous big roan.

They came to burn Lawrence,
They came not to stay,
Jim Lane he was up
At the break of the day,
He saw them a-coming
And got in the right,
Then crawled in a corn crib
To get out of sight.

Oh, Quantrill's a fighter,
A bold-hearted boy,
A brave man or woman,
He'd never annoy,
He'd take from the wealthy
And give it to the poor,
For brave men there's never
A bolt to his door.

THE RAMBLING BOY

"Another man's life don't make a soft pillow at night."

Marriage can be bliss or purgatory, take your pick. This poor fellow claims his wife *made* him steal to support her. Of Irish or English origin, this ballad has been collected as "The Flash Lad," "In Newry Town," and "The Robber." In this version he is a "rake," while in others he is "rich," or "rude."

It's there I married me a wife,
I loved her dearer than I did my life.
I treated her both kind and gay,
She caused me to rob the road highway.

I robbed them all, I do declare,
I robbed them all in deep despair.
I robbed them of ten thousand pounds,
One night when I was a-rambling around.

I'll buy me a ticket for Greenville town,
I'll get on the train and I'll sit down.
The wheels will roll and the whistle will blow,
In five more days I'll be at home.

My mother said she weeps and mourns,
My sister says she's left alone.
My own true love in deep despair,
With a pale red ribbon in her curly brown hair.

I have dry goods to carry me through,
Three glittering swords and a pistol too.
And a pretty fair girl for to pay my toll,
With her diamond rings & her silver & gold.

When I'm dead and in my grave,
No more good liquor will I crave.
On my tombstone I want it wrote,
Ten thousand gallons went down my throat.

> "If a man drinks he's liable to go home and steal his own pants." A Tombstone saying

CLAY, BUTCH & WILD BILL

Fancy Shooting

Wild Bill Hickok was once asked if he was as good a shot as legend said he was. Wild Bill drew his pistols, one in each hand, and pointed to the eaves of the two-story frame building across the street. "See that knot hole? I'll stitch a button hole around it." And he fanned ten shots, the ten leads made a circle around the hole.[1]

Butch Cassidy

Butch Cassidy was known for his generosity, laughter, and love of practical jokes. After entering a Wyoming saloon, he noticed a local drunk asleep in a chair tipped against the wall. Butch first shot out the rungs out of the chair one by one, and then shot the tips of the legs until it collapsed while still holding its slumbering occupant. Butch's custom was to award the objects of his practical jokes a twenty-dollar gold piece. History doesn't recollect whether the drunk woke up in time to collect his prize.[15]

Courtesy of Jim Bob Tinsley

WILD BILL HICKOK

A Grave Agreement

Tales of Clay Allison were legendary in Oklahoma in the 1870's. He once fought a knife duel with a man named Johnson in an open grave they had dug. They agreed that the loser would remain in the grave, and the winner would cover it up. Johnson stayed behind.

"He punished the air with his singing."

ROSE CONNALLY

Raised a pet, but gone wild.[11]

The murderer of Rose Connally left only one clue behind, this song. From it we can begin to track the rascal. To confuse his pursuers, his song became known as "Down in the Willow Gardens," which is where he freely admitted he committed his evil crime. In one version of the song, he stabbed her with his "skeever," another has him using a saber, while in a third it was a dagger. Perhaps to further confuse us, he variously names himself Patsey O'Reilly, Morrison or Pattimaredo. His last clue is a real doosey. He admitted poisoning his victim either with "Merkley" wine, Burgundy wine, or Burglar's wine.

Coroner's Report

"Came to his death by suicide. At a distance of one hundred and fifty yards he tried to shoot a man who was armed with a Winchester rifle."

Outright Insult: He didn't have manners
enough to carry guts to a bear.[24]

"I popped him between the horns an' knocked his jaw back so far he could scratch the back of his neck with his front teeth."[12]

I drew my saber through her
Which was a bloody knife.
I threw her in the river,
Which was a dreadful sight.

My father always taught me
That money would set me free.
If I would murder that pretty little miss
Whose name was Rose Connally.

He's sitting now at his own cabin door,
A-wiping his weeping eyes.
A-looking at his own dear son,
Upon the scaffold high.

My race is run beneath the sun,
Though hell's now waiting for me.
For I did murder that pretty little miss
Whose name was Rose Connally.

Warning: Be careful in singing this song under the window of a certain New York publisher using the words "Burgundy wine." One publisher was threatened with a hefty copyright lawsuit when he printed this song using the words "Burgundy wine." But then, if you sing Burglar's wine, you might get arrested for being a robber!

Outright Insult: He was built like a snake on stilts.

ROY BEAN

"There's no Sunday west of Kansas City."

It was often a fine line between outlaws and lawmen. A case in point was Roy Bean, who proclaimed himself, "The Law West of the Pecos." Bean's qualification for dispensing instant and arbitrary justice included experience as a bull-whacker, blockade-runner, wood merchant and saloon-keeper. In 1882, he shrewdly got himself appointed justice of the peace of what he called Langtry, Texas. Judge Bean quickly opened for business a combined saloon and courtroom, which was known as the Jersey Lily. His specialty was "fine-able" penalties, with all of the fines going directly into his own pockets.

"Hear ye, Hear ye! This honorable court's now in session and if any of you galoots wants a snort afore we start, let him step up to the bar and name his pizen."

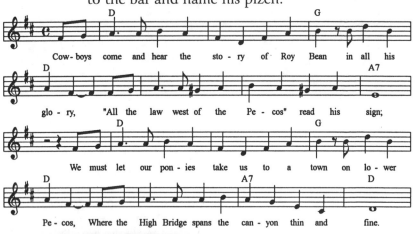

Cow-boys come and hear the sto-ry of Roy Bean in all his glo-ry, "All the law west of the Pe-cos" read his sign; We must let our pon-ies take us to a town on lo-wer Pe-cos, Where the High Bridge spans the can-yon thin and fine.

JUDGE ROY BEAN, ON PORCH WITH HAT.

"The deceased came to his death at the hands of an unknown party who was a damned good pistol shot." Judge Roy Bean

ROY BEAN

"Talk is cheap but it takes money to buy whiskey."

He was born one day near Toyah where he learned to be a lawyer
And a teacher and a barber and the Mayor.
He was cook and old shoe-mender, sometimes preacher and bartender,
And it costs two bits to have him cut your hair.

He was right smart of a hustler, and considerable a rustler,
And at mixing up an eggnog he was grand.
He was clever, he was merry, he could drink a Tom and Jerry,
On occasion at a round-up took a hand.

Though the story isn't funny, there was once he had no money
Which was for him not very strange or rare,
So he went to help Pap Wyndid, but he got so absentminded
That he put his RB brand on old Pap's steer.

As Pap was right smart angry, old Roy Bean went down to Langtry
Where he opened up an office and a store.
There he'd sell you a drink or buttons or another rancher's muttons
Though the latter made the other fellow sore.

Once there came from Austin city a young dude reported witty
Out of Bean he sort of guessed he'd take a rise.
And he got unusually frisky as he up and called for whisky
Saying, "Bean, now hurry up, goldurn your eyes."

Then a'down he threw ten dollars, which the same Roy quickly collars,
Then the same Roy holds to nine and hands back one,
So the stranger gave a holler as he saw that single dollar
And at that began the merriment and fun.

The dude he slammed the table just as hard as he was able,
That the price of whiskey was too high he swore,
Said Roy Bean, "For all that fussin' and your most outrageous cussin'
You are fined the other dollar by the law."

The Dead Man's Hand
When Wild Bill Hickok was killed by a shot in the back of the head by Jack McCall in a Deadwood saloon, the hand of cards he was playing has since been called, "The Dead Man's Hand," two black aces and two black eights.

ROY BEAN

"You rancid, left-handed old parallelogram, you."[2]

"On this place I owe a lease, sir, I'm the Justice of the peace, sir,
The Law west of the Pecos all is here,
And you've acted very badly." Then the dude went off sadly
While down his lily cheek there rolled a tear.

One fine day they found a dead man who in life had been a redman,
So it's doubtless he was nothing else than bad,
They called Bean to view the body, first he took a drink of toddy,
Then he listed all the things the dead man had.

JUDGE ROY BEAN

For a redman he was tony for he had a pretty pony,
And a dandy bit and saddle and a rope,
He'd a fine Navajo rug and a quart within his jug
And a bronco that was dandy on the lope.

So the find it was quite rare-o, for he'd been a "cocinero,"
And his payday hadn't been so far away,
He'd a bran' new fine white Stetson & a silver Smith and Wesson
While a purse of forty dollars jingled gay.

Said Roy Bean, "You'll learn a lesson for you have a Smith and Wesson,
And to carry implements of war is very wrong.
Forty dollars I will fine you, for we couldn't well confine you
As already you've been laying round too long."

So you boys have heard the story of Roy Bean in all his glory,
He's the man who was the Justice and the Law
He was handy with his hooks, he was orn'ry in his looks,
And just now I ain't a-telling any more.

A horse thief had been arrested, tried and, after much debate, was found to be innocent by a jury. The jury filed back into the courtroom and the foreman made his speech. It took him over an hour to tell in fancy oratory that the defendant had been found innocent of all charges. But the judge shook his head.

"You'll have to reconsider," he said. "The defendant was hung a couple of hours ago."[7]

THE LEGENDS OF SAM BASS

"If a man knows anything, he ought to die with it in him."
Sam Bass' last words.

Legends die hard. Even before Sam Bass met a Texas Ranger's bullet, legends told that Sam had secretly buried large amounts of gold and silver around Denton, Texas. Treasure hunters, armed with "authentic maps," shovels, and even divining rods, fanned out all over Texas looking for buried chests of Sam's gold. Fueled by rumors and gossip, tales of secret hiding places circulated for over 50 years.

Stories of Sam's generosity were not even considered legend, but *fact*. Once, while on the run, Sam asked a man on a fresh mount to trade horses with him. When he refused, Sam said, "Do you know who I am? I am Sam Bass." With that, the man leaped off his horse and began running for his life. Sam called him back, and after changing saddles, handed the surprised man seventy-five dollars.

SAM BASS

One time Sam stopped a rancher in Dallas County, Texas and asked for some chewing tobacco. "You can buy more, but I can't," Sam said. The cowman handed over his plug, and after cutting off a piece, Sam returned what was left, along with a half dollar. Sam then offered to buy the man's horse for fifty dollars. When the man said he had only paid twenty-five dollars for the nag, Sam suggested he throw in his old mule for boot, and both men rode away smiling.

Though Sam Bass was a robber, a gambler, and a whiskey guzzler, his acts of generosity earned Sam the respect of local citizens. As his own ballad says, "A kinder-hearted fellow, you seldom ever see."

Outright Insult: He was uglier than a new-sheared sheep.[12]

SAM BASS

"Wild and woolly, hard to curry."[11]

They say the ballad "Sam Bass" was written by John Denton of Gainesville, Texas about 1879. Some cowboys swore the song helped calm more herds moving north to Kansas cowtowns than any other cowboy ballad.

Sam Bass was born in In-di-an-a, it was his na-tive home. And at the age of sev-en-teen young Sam be-gan to roam. He first went out to Tex-as, a cow-boy for to be, A kin-der-heart-ed fel-low you sel-dom ev-er see.

Sam used to deal in race stock, one called the "Denton mare."
He matched her in scrub races and took her to the air.
He used to coin the money and spent it just as free,
He always drank good whiskey wherever he might be.

Sam Bass had four companions, all bold and daring lads.
They were Underwood and Jackson, Joel Collins and Old Dad.
More bold and reckless cowboys the Wild West never knew,
They whipped the Texas Rangers and chased the boys in blue.

Young Sam he left the Collins ranch in the merry month of May,
With a herd of Texas cattle for the Black Hills far away.
Sold out in Custer City, and then went on a spree,
With a harder set of cowboys you seldom ever see.

On the way back down to Texas, they robbed the U.P. train,
They then split up in couples and started out again.
Joel Collins and his partner were overtaken soon,
With all their hard-earned money, they had to meet their doom.

> "Every one of my hangings was a scientific job."
> George Maledon, known as "The Prince of Hangmen."[1]

SAM BASS

"Cinch up a little, your saddle's slippin'."[12]

Sam made it back to Texas, all right side up with care,
Rode in the town of Denton with all his friends to share.
But his stay was short in Texas, three robberies did he do,
He robbed the Longview passenger, express, and mail cars too.

Sam had another comrade, called "Arkansas" for short,
Killed by a Texas Ranger by the name of Thomas Floyd.
Jim Murphy was arrested and then released on bail,
He jumped his bond at Tyler and took the train for Terrell.

But Major Jones had posted Jim and that was all a stall.
It was only a plan to capture Sam before the coming fall.
He met his fate at Round Rock, July the twenty-first,
They pierced poor Sam with rifle balls and emptied out his purse.

Sam Bass he is a corpse now and six feet under clay,
And Jackson's in the bushes a-trying to get away.
Murphy borrowed Sam's hard money and didn't want to pay,
The only way he saw to win was give poor Sam away.

And so he sold out Sam and Barns and left their friends to mourn.
Oh, what a scorching Jim will get when Gabriel blows his horn!
Perhaps he got to heaven, there's none of us can say,
But if I'm right in my surmise, he's gone the other way.

Gun Nick-Names

*Old Rackatee,
Smoke Wagon,
Old Betsy,
Life Preserver,
Tiger, Old Blue,
Talkin' Iron,
Hardware,
Shootin' Iron,
Blue Lightnin',
Equalizer,
Persuader,
Hog-Leg,
Thumb-Buster,
Artillery,
Flame-Thrower,
Lead-Pusher.*[12]

A Cure For Snoring

John Wesley Harden, noted outlaw, once cured a man of snoring. One night he was awakened by the snoring in the adjacent hotel room. Harden fired his six-gun in the direction of the snores, which quickly ceased, providing all the guests with a quiet night's sleep.

Outright Insult: His lip hangs down like a blacksmith's apron.[12]

THE LEGEND OF STAGOLEE

"Trouble is a rat-tailed hoss tied short at fly-time."

His real name was Stack Lee, but they all called him Stagolee. At birth, a fortune teller was summoned because the newborn was double-jointed and had a full set of teeth. What worried the fortune teller most was that he was born with a veil over his face, a sign that Stagolee would come to no good.

The fortune teller's warnings all came true. One day, the devil carried Stagolee off to the graveyard. Knowing his weakness for fine Stetson hats, the devil bought his soul in exchange for a magic oxblood Stetson hat made from a man-eating panther that the devil himself had skinned alive. As long as Stagolee wore that hat, he had magical powers:

He could crawl into a bottle on a shelf.
He could walk barefoot on a hot slag from a pig iron furnace.
He could turn himself into a horse and gallop away.
He could eat hot fire without getting singed.
He could change himself into a mountain or a varmint.
He wore no shoes and his footprint was that of a horse.

The devil, meanwhile, was growing impatient for Stagolee's soul. One cold frosty evening Stagolee was having a big winning streak down at the Jack 'O Diamonds in St Louis. In his haste of raking in all the money, Stagolee hung his magic Stetson on the back of his chair. The devil, seeing his chance, quickly turned himself into Billy Lyons, an innocent family man. Grabbing Stagolee's prized Stetson, he tore out the double doors toward the White Elephant Barrel House with Stagolee in hot pursuit. When Stagolee saw the real Billy Lyons, he killed him for stealing his magic Stetson. The devil was sorely disappointed that the police did not kill Stagolee right then and there for the judge sentenced Stack to 75 years in the Jefferson Pen. When the devil finally claimed his prize, Stagolee became quite popular in hell, where he played guitar in a jazz band with the devil himself on cornet.

> Outright Insult: He was popular as a wet dog at a parlor social.

STAGOLEE

"Whiskey'll make a new man out of you.
But then HE has to have a drink."

Stag - o - lee was a bad— man, Eve - ry - bo - dy knows,— Spent one hun - dred dol - lars Just to buy him a suit of clothes— He's a bad— man, that cruel— Stag - o - lee—

'Twas on a Christmas morning,
The hour was about ten,
When Stagolee shot Billy Lyons,
And landed in the Jefferson Pen,
He's a bad man, that cruel Stagolee.

"Jailer, Oh jailer,
I can't seem to sleep;
For the ghost of Billy Lyons
'Round my bed does mourn and weep"
He's a bad man, that cruel Stagolee.

All the devil's little children
Went scramblin' up the wall,
Saying, "Catch him, please papa,
Before he kills us all,"
He's a bad man, that cruel Stagolee.

Stack he told the devil,
"Come on, let's have some fun,"
You stick me with your pitchfork,
I'll shoot you with my .41,"
He's a bad man, that cruel Stagolee.

Stagolee says, "Now Mister Devil,
Me'n you's gonna have some fun
You play the cornet,
Betty Black beat the drum,"
He's a bad man, that cruel Stagolee.

Stagolee took the pitchfork,
And he laid it on the shelf
"Stand back, Tom Devil,
I'm gonna rule Hell by myself,"
He's a bad man, that cruel Stagolee.

A Tombstone lawyer was pleading his case to a jury in Judge Wells Spicer's court when a burro beneath the window started braying loudly. Lawyer Marcus A. Smith arose and gravely said, "If it please the court, I object to the two attorneys speaking at the same time."[16]

A half pint of whiskey was like an inch of cordwood or an ounce of cornshucks.

> "A drunk is like a whiskey-bottle,
> all neck and belly and no head."

Vamoose!!!

A horse thief was arrested and released on bail. His lawyer knew he was guilty as sin and that the jury surely would hang him. Not one to mince words, the lawyer told his client:

"You haven't got the chance of a snowball in hell. All the evidence is against you. You best skip out of here."

The man looked bewildered.

"Don't you understand???" said the lawyer. "The only way for you to save your neck is to vamoose!! Get away from here as fast as you can! And don't come back!"

"You mean I ought to go somewhere else?" asked his client. "That's what I've been trying to tell you! Get out of here as quick as you can!" "But," asked the horse thief, "Where can I go? Ain't I already in Texas?"[4]

TEXAS RANGERS

NOTICE!
To Thieves, Thugs, Fakers
And Bunko-Steerers,
Among Whom Are
J.J. Harlin, alias "Off Wheeler," Saw Dust
Charlie, Wm. Hedges, Billy the Kid,
Billy Mullin, Little Jack, The Cuter,
Pock-Marked Kid, and about Twenty Others:
If Found within the Limits of this City after
TEN O'CLOCK P.M. this Night,
you will be Invited to attend a
GRAND NECK-TIE PARTY
The Expense of which will be born by
1000 SUBSTANTIAL CITIZENS
Las Vegas, March 24, 1881

Outright Insult: He looked like the hindquarters of bad luck.[24]

TOM DULA

"If inlaws were outlawed, only outlaws would have inlaws."

The ballad of "Tom Dula" has all the ingredients of a classic outlaw ballad: murder, mystery, an eternal love triangle, taking secrets to the grave, the Devil, ghosts and even fiddle playing!

Tom Dula had fought bravely for the Confederacy under Zebulon Vance's 26th North Carolina Regiment. On his return, Tom quickly established a reputation as a reckless desperado who terrorized his neighbors. The community where Tom lived near the banks of the Yadkin River was no Garden of Eden. According to the *New York Herald*: "Such a state of immorality prevails among these people and such a general system of free-loveism prevails, that it is a wise child that knows its father."

Tom was soon courting Laura Foster, described as very beautiful, with chestnut curls, merry blue eyes and "wild as a buck." Before long, Tom had turned his fancy to Ann Melton. One old-timer remembered Ann as "The prettiest woman I ever looked in the face of." To the horror of Tom and Ann, Tom discovered he had caught a social disease from Laura and had given it to Ann. For this they swore vengeance. At their trial, it was charged that Tom and Ann had dug a shallow grave, and together had murdered Laura. After a second trial, Tom was found guilty and sentenced to hang, but declared that, "I am the only person that had a hand in the murder of Laura Foster." At her own trial, Ann Melton is said to have said, "A rope will never go around this pearly white neck." In fact, Ann *was* acquitted. According to one old-timer, "She'd a been hung, but her neck was just too pretty to stretch hemp." He added, "If there'd been 'ary woman on the jury, she'd a got first degree. Men couldn't look at the woman and keep their heads." Even Zebulon Vance, who defended Dula, admitted "He was shielding a woman, who really committed the murder, but Dula never talked."

Unwritten Law: Always drink your whiskey with your gun hand, to show your friendly intentions.

TOM DULA

"He was too proud to cut hay an' not wild 'nough to eat it."[12]

They say Tom's friends brought his banjo to him in jail, where he composed a ballad about the murder. Others say he rode to the gallows on his own coffin, while playing the fiddle. He was hung May 1, 1868.

Stories also abound about the death of Ann Melton. Some claim that as she lay dying, she made a last-minute confession to her husband, who never revealed the content of her confession. Others say the Devil carried her off and as she lay dying, blue flames crackled around her bed. Some say that you could see squalling black cats running up and down the walls of her room, and you could hear the sound of frying meat. Others say on her death-bed she screamed in agony, "Take him away, the big black man in the corner, the one with the pitchfork!"

Legends tell that on spring nights on the glen where Col. Jim Horton found the body of Laura Foster, a ghostly ball of blue white fire rises to the sky. They say it is the ghost of Laura Foster, still searching for her false lover.

Hang your head, Tom Du-la Hang your head and cry, You killed poor Laura Fos-ter And now you're bound to die.

Outright Insult: He was so thin he could take a bath in a shotgun barrel.[12]

TOM DULA

Outlaw Threat: "I'll kick yo' pants up 'round your neck so tight they'll choke you to death."[12]

You took her by the roadside where you begged to be excused,
You took her by the roadside where there you hid her shoes.
You took her on the hillside to make her your wife,
You took her on the hillside where there you took her life.

I dug her grave four feet long, I dug it three feet deep,
And throwed the cold clay over her, and tromped it with my feet.
Take down my own violin and play it all you please,
For at this time tomorrow, it'll be no use to me.

This world and one more, then where do you reckon I'll be,
If it hadn't of been for Grayson, I'd a been in Tennessee.
At this time tomorrow, where do you reckon I'll be?
Way down yonder in a holler, a-hanging from a white oak tree.

Jes' Like Stringing Fish

Pat Dooling, the fearless Texas Ranger, was once asked if he was ever scared in the face of danger. "Yes," he answered. "One time in West Texas, I crossed a bunch of outlaws, and they sent me word that they'd kill me on sight. That scared me, for it was a bad bunch, all man-killers, and I knowed they meant it, and I kept my eyes open for them.

One day I rode into a new town and stopped to water my horse. Seeing a saloon, I lit and went in for a drink. The saloon had a long bar, with a short end bar at right angles to it. I stepped up to this short bar and asked for my drink. Just then I looked down along the long bar, and there stood that outlaw bunch, five of them. I looked right into their faces and they looked into mine. From where I stood at the end bar, the five were all in range in a straight line ahead of me, and by good luck I got my six-shooter out a leetle ahead of any of them." A long pause followed.

"Well, what happened then?" asked the excited listener.

"It was just like stringin' fish." And that was all he said.[1]

Frontier Wisdom: Never ride a horse named "Buck."

Tom Sherman's Barroom

Seventeen men claimed to be the "original" Jesse James.

Finding the origins of "Tom Sherman's Barroom" is about as easy as tracking a whisper through a blizzard. We do know it started out as "The Unfortunate Rate," a popular Irish ballad from 1790 about a soldier who contracted a "social disease" from a prostitute who followed the army from camp to camp. From there it traveled to England, where it was known as "The Bad Girl's Lament." It then became the sailor's song, "Tarpaulin Jacket," and during the Crimean War was known as "The Soldier's Lament." By the 1870's, it was taken up by American cowboys as "The Cowboy's Lament," or "The Streets of Laredo." In the cowboy version, the poor lad died not of venereal disease, but from drinking and gambling. "Tom Sherman's Barroom" also shows the influence of "St. James Hospital," "St. James Infirmary," "One Morning in May," and "Those Gambler's Blues."

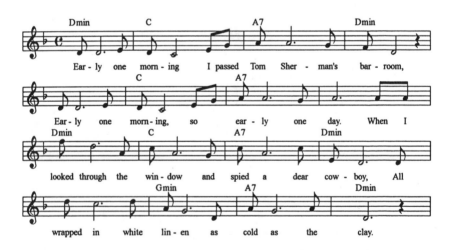

> A man was accused of stealing gold in Tonopah, Nevada. "Guilty or not guilty?" thundered the judge. "Gosh, your honor, I don't know," answered the man. "I ain't heard the evidence yet."[2]

"This saloon's so bad, a rattlesnake'd be ashamed to meet his mother."

TOM SHERMAN'S BARROOM

"He told lies so well a man would be a fool not to believe them."

"Come Papa and Mama, and sit ye down by me.
Come sit down beside me and sing me a song,
For my poor head is achin' & my sad heart is breakin'
I'm a poor cowboy and knowed I done wrong."

"Once in the saddle I used to go dashing,
Once in the saddle I used to go gay.
But I first took to drinkin', and then to card playin',
I am a poor cowboy, and dyin' today."

"Get sixteen young cowboys to carry my coffin,
Get sixteen pretty maidens to sing me a song.
Put bunches of roses all over my coffin,
Put roses to deaden the clods as they fall."

"Well, beat the drum slowly and play the fifes lowly
Play the Dead March as they carry me along.
Take me to the graveyard and lay the sod o'er me,
For I'm a poor cowboy, and I know I done wrong."

Henry Starr once robbed a bank, walked three miles out of town, and was eating supper at a farmer's house when the telephone rang. Answering it, the farmer turned to Starr and said, "The sheriff says the bank was held up and he wants to know if I've seen a suspicious character out this way." "Tell him the robber is at your house eating supper and for him to come on out and get me." With that, he finished his meal, paid for it, and left.[1]

Black Jack Ketchum had just one request before he was hanged: "Can't you hurry this up a bit? I hear they eat dinner in Hades at twelve sharp and I don't aim to be late."[9]

WILD BILL JONES

"They made an ordinary fight look like a prayer meetin'."

The only thing Wild Bill Jones left for us to remember him by was this song. Though we've tracked him from North Carolina all the way to Arkansas, his identity remains a mystery. You can sing the indented verse as a chorus.

As— I— walked— out— for to take a lit tle
He was walk in' and a talk in' by my true— lov er's

walk.— I walked up on that Wild— Bill Jones.—
side.— I bid— him to leave— her alone.—

He said my age it is twenty-one,
Too old for to be controlled.
I brought my revolver from my side,
And I destroyed that poor boy's soul.

So pass around that long neck bottle,
And we'll all go on a spree.
For today was the last of that Wild Bill Jones,
And tomorrow is the last of me.

He reeled & he staggered & he fell to the ground,
And he gave one dying groan.
I put my arms around my darlin' neck,
Saying "Baby, won't you please come home?"

They sent me to prison for twenty long years,
This poor boy longs to be free.
But Wild Bill Jones and that long neck bottle,
Has made a ruin of me.

I was on that train when she whistled for night,
I was on her when she whistled for day.
She come around the curve and strained every nerve,
That old engine's gonna carry me away.

> "We never did hang the wrong one but once or twice," said one judge. "And them fellers needed to be hung anyhow jes' on general principles."[5]

THANKS!

"Thrusting my nose firmly between his teeth, I threw him heavily to the ground on top of me." Mark Twain

Three cheers to the posse for helping to round up the outlaws. Barbara Swell, Annie, Wes & Rita Erbsen, Lori & John Erbsen, Carol Elizabeth Jones, Norm Cohen, Jim Bob Tinsley, Will Pruett, Alvin Prince, Henry Queen, Dave Freeman, Kinney Rorrer, Jean Harrison, Bucky Hanks, Peggy Seeger, Bob Willoughby, Janet Swell Webb, Joe Bruno, Emily Hazelwood, and Rik & Bonnie Neustein. Thanks to Tracy McMahon for cover concept and Steve Millard for cover art.

CREDITS

[1] *Hands Up!* Fred Ellsworth Sutton, 1927, [2] *The Home Book of Western Humor*, ed. Philip H. Ault, [3] *The New Mexico Candle*, B.A. Botkin, [4] *Folk Laughter on the American Frontier*, Mody C. Boatright, [5] *The Story of the Cowboy*, Emerson Hugh, 1897, [6] *Heldorado*, William A. Brechenridge, 1928, [7] *Humor of the American Cowboy*, Stan Hoig, 1958, [8] *Idaho Lore*, Federal Writers' Project, 1939, [9] *The Bad Man of the West*, George Hendricks, 1942, [10] *Cowboy Lore*, Jules Verne Allen, [11] *Texas and Southwestern Lore*, Ed J. Frank Dobie, [12] *Cowboy Lingo*, Ramon F. Adams, 1936, [13] *The Cowboy and His Humor*, Ramon F. Adams, [14] *Desert Scrap Book*, [15] *Powder River*, Struthers Burt, [16] *The Illustrated Life and Times of Wyatt Earp*, Bob Bose Bell, 1994, [17] *The Authentic Wild West*, James D. Horan, 1977, [18] *Glamorous Days*, Frank H. Buchick, 1934, [19] *The Badmen*, Goddard Lieberson, 1963, [20] *Ballads and Songs of the Frontier Folk*, J. Frank Dobie, [21] *Writer's Guide to Everyday Life in the 1800's*, Mark McCutcheon, 1993, [22] *Railroadman*, Chauncey Del French, 1938. [23] *West Virginia Heritage Recipes*, 1976 , [24] *Folklore on the American Land*, Duncan Emrick, 1972.

BAT'S LAST WORDS

"There are many in this old world of ours who hold that things break about even for all of us. I have observed, for example, that we all get about the same amount of ice. The rich get it in the summer time and the poor get it in the winter time."[1]

The last words of Bat Masterson, who fell not in a gunfight but at his desk in New York City.

Outlaw Superstitions

Outlaws, who were afraid of little else, were curiously superstitious about one thing: dying with their boots on. The dying request of countless outlaws was to remove their boots before they died. Many pleaded with authorities not to forward the news to their mothers that they had died with their boots on.

Wayne Erbsen

Guitar Chords

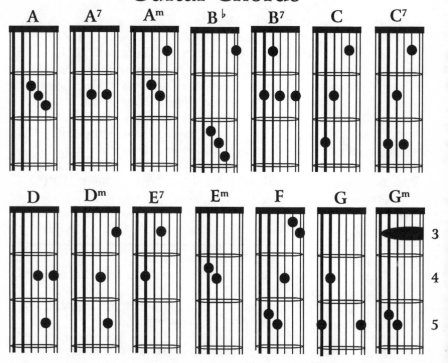

He didnt know how many beans made five.[24]